ETERNALLY MINDED MAMAS

ONE-MONTH DEVOTIONAL AND JOURNAL

Setting Our Mothering Eyes on Christ
One Day-at-a-Time

Katie LaPierre

Praise for Eternally Minded Mamas
One-Month Devotional and Journal

"What Katie LaPierre has given to you is a gift of love. We all need others who are traveling the same road and understand the joys and the trials. As you read Eternally Minded Mamas, you'll be empowered to face your challenges with courage as you focus first on the Word of God and take up your sword of faith for your highest calling - motherhood."

Jacqueline Franks—Founder of DeepRootsatHome.com

"In this beautiful gem of a mother's devotional you will find encouragement to press onward in the mothering journey for the glory of God. You will be reminded that Biblical, fruitful mothering is only possible when our weakness is exchanged for His strength. I could relate to Katie's honesty in sharing the struggles of motherhood and felt inspired by the hope she offers, rooted strongly in the Word of God and gospel truth. This book is a beautiful reminder that all the effort and sacrifices are worth it in light of eternity!"

Ruth Adams—Author of *Legacy: Reflections of a Homeschooled Homeschooling Mama* and Founder of LegacyHomeschoolReflections.com

"Scripture soaked, transparent, genuine and COMPLETELY relatable! You are going to find yourself groaning and amen-ing as you search your heart through each day of this devotional! Katie's desire to be eternally minded in every area—including mothering—will resonate with and encourage your heart! I love that she only points to herself to show the reality of this earthly struggle, but shines the light on Christ and His power as our daily source for fulfilling the high calling of motherhood. 'God is our refuge and strength...' Psalm 46:1. I can see this being a well-worn, treasured resource of encouragement for years to come in my own personal prayer closet."

Shelley Mitchell—Pastor's Wife and Revive Our Hearts Ambassador

"Katie LaPierre brings a devotional tailored made for busy moms who long to get more of the Word in their lives. Sharing candidly from her own life as a mom of many, she points out how our perspective as mothers needs to stem from Scripture. By bringing light to verses that can be implemented in the midst of daily mothering chaos and real life, this devotional isn't merely idle theory. It will challenge you, uplift you, and sharpen your vision toward living out godly mothering!"

Brook Wayne—Itinerant Speaker's Wife, Co-Founder of FamilyRenewal.org, and co-author of *Pitchin' a Fit! Overcoming Angry and Stressed-out Parenting.*

"Katie LaPierre has written many inspiring things in this book. But the most inspirational thing of all is the way she lives. I have watched Katie parent her children with gentleness and understanding, relying on the Lord's strength during long days after short nights. She continues to shine with the joy of the Lord, and her husband and children are blessed indeed. Read her book. It's like having a long talk with Katie. You'll be blessed!"

Lois Green—Pastor's Wife and Missionary

Having read many devotionals dedicated to Mothers I will say that there is a crucial ingredient missing from many: "Confrontation with grace." As in, yes the Lord is for us but how can we as mothers confront our sinfulness without getting offended, and feel his over abundance of grace? This is why I absolutely loved this devotional. It wasn't all flowers and rainbows, it was flowers, rainbows, and a challenge to seek the Lord in all things motherhood. It's definitely a devotional for a mama who wants to grow in Christ.

Ana Nelson—Founder of SheFoundGrace.com

"What an excellent reminder of what a devotion to God should look like! I was blessed by Katie's consistent, compassionate plea for us to return to the Word, and to the beautiful plan God has for our daily walk as mothers. She spoke with grace and a purpose I know comes from holding tightly to Jesus herself. Thank you for your willingness to speak what He has taught you, and continues to teach you, Katie."

Meg Dickey—Wife and Mother

Eternally Minded Mamas
One-Month Devotional and Journal

Eternally Minded Mamas
One-Month Devotional and Journal

*Setting Our Mothering Eyes on
Christ One Day at a Time*

Katie LaPierre

www.katielapierre.org | www.scottlapierre.org

ISBN: 0-9995551-2-X

ISBN 13: 978-0-9995551-2-5

Library of Congress Control Number: 2018915095

Charis Family Publishing

Dedication

This devotional is dedicated to all the Christian women pouring out their lives for their husbands, children, homes, and Savior.

Thank you for all you do. I count myself blessed to provide you even a little encouragement.

Love,
Katie

Foreword

Second only to the Lord Himself, who knows Katie best? Me! Her husband, Scott. I could encourage you to read this devotional because my wife is a deeply spiritual woman who knows God's Word well, and her thoughts will richly bless you. But honestly, would that separate this work from most other devotionals? Probably not. So what makes this one unique? Why should you read it, versus the thousands of others available? In two words: the trenches.

My wife is in them! We have seven children, eleven and under. She knows your struggles. She lives them every day! Occasionally, functions take Katie away, and then I try to fill her shoes. Whenever that happens, my appreciation and respect for her soar. I constantly ask myself, "How can my wife do this every day?" This devotional is born out of her regular labor for our kids, me, and her Lord.

Katie is also a senior pastor's wife. In Genesis 2:18, God said, "It is not good that the man should be alone; I will make him a helper fit for him." One primary way Katie helps me in my role is by going over the sermon with me twice each week. Everyone at Woodland Christian Church knows how invaluable this is to me. More times than they can count, they have heard me say, "When Katie and I were going over the sermon together…" I can't tell you how much I benefit from Katie's spiritual insight. Many times when I receive positive comments about sermons, if I reply honestly, I must say, "Those were Katie's thoughts." In this devotional, you'll benefit from the same spiritual insight that has helped my preaching week-after-week.

A few days ago Katie said, "I feel like I should be investing more in some of the women in our church." My initial thought was, "Your plate is already so full with our kids, the house, and the ways you help me. How can you think of more?" She can think of more because she has a deep burden for other women in the trenches. You! Katie wrote this devotional because she loves you, and has a sincere desire to encourage you as an *Eternally Minded Mama*.

In Christ,
Scott LaPierre
Katie's Husband, Senior Pastor, Author, and Speaker

Contents

Introduction

Hello Mama,

I'm so glad you have this devotional in your hands. I have been praying and will continue to pray the Lord uses it greatly in your mothering journey. It's a hard journey, isn't it? But a worthy journey when we walk it with the King of kings.

A little about me: I have believed Jesus died for me since seventh grade, but I did not live for Him until I was twenty. Since then I have walked with Him through the hills and valleys, but I never imagined I would be a pastor's wife and homeschooling seven children, eleven and under. Honestly, every day is a struggle. I have felt despair and been emotionally, physically, and mentally drained. Many times I have poured out my heart to Scott (and the Lord). I've shared I don't want to keep doing this. That may not sound beautiful or appealing, but it's truthful. Do you want real transparency and vulnerability? Here's a message I sent Scott JUST last night when I was up nursing Ruby:

> I'm so discouraged right now. So tired and she will not sleep. Pray for me, honey. I just don't see how I can keep doing this, stay sane, and keep a home, and not worry about my baby who isn't growing…all while not sleeping.

You can probably guess it didn't occur to me last night when I sent this that it would be in the Introduction of my devotional, but what better way for you to see what I'm going through too?

I started an online ministry a few years ago called Eternally Minded Mamas because my heart is to encourage other women. I don't want to put my best fake foot forward. I want to strengthen you in the mess, because—let's face it—motherhood is messy!

Maybe you are struggling too? My devotions in the following pages have been produced from a heart of struggle seeking God's help through His Word. I hope you can see Him, draw closer to Him, and gain the encouragement you need in your journey as you read and journal.

Love,
Katie

Day 1—Faithful Mothering

*"Whatever you do, work heartily, as for the Lord and not for men,
knowing that from the Lord you will receive the inheritance as your reward.
You are serving the Lord Christ."*
—*Colossians 3:23–24*

I send my children on errands throughout the day. "Go grab this." "Take this downstairs." "Go brush your hair." "Take this dirty laundry to the hamper."

You know what's sad? Some of my kids are more faithful than others. I can count on some of my kids to do what I told them and then return to what they are supposed to be doing or check in with me to see if there is anything else I need. Sometimes they are faithful to do the job all the way, and other times they do the bare minimum. They are often hard to rely on. They are prone to wander and getting distracted. I never know if they will actually follow through.

Which child are you like to your Father?

He has called you to run His errands here on earth. You are His ambassador. You are His hands and feet. Are you faithful to walk in what He has called you to? Will you hear: "Well done good and faithful servant?" (Matthew 25:23). Are you likely to finish the tasks He lays before you well and completely or haphazardly and with mediocrity?

Don't despair. God's grace is always there. He can keep you faithful as you depend on Him and stay immersed in His Word. We are all prone to wander, but He is prone to faithfulness. As we unite ourselves with Him, we are bound to be the one He can count on as we rely on His strength to carry us through.

In your journaling entry, ask the Lord to show you where you have been mediocre in your work for Him. Write down three ways you will strive to work faithfully for Him today where you are tempted to slack.

*"For we are His workmanship,
created in Christ Jesus for good works,
which God prepared beforehand,
that we should walk in them."*
—*Ephesians 2:10*

Journal Notes

_____

_____

_____

_____

_____

_____

_____

_____

_____

_____

_____

_____

_____

Day 2—Peaceful Mothering

"Rejoice always, pray without ceasing, give thanks in all circumstances;
for this is the will of God in Christ Jesus for you."
—1 Thessalonians 5:16–18

A peaceful home is one where the mama is pleasant when circumstances are not—where a mama chooses to smile when children cry. The mama truly sets the tone. We don't rise above the chaos because we are so amazing but because our God is and out of our love for Him, we obey Him.

The wise woman builds her home, but the foolish one tears it down. Choose to build up and not tear down one moment at a time. One spilled cup of milk at a time. One tantrum at a time. One sibling squabble at a time. One sickness at a time. One bill at a time. One early morning or late night at a time.

The wise woman is always looking for times to build up and seek peace while the foolish one is always drowning in self-pity and can't see past her trials.

The Lord is with you, Mama, and can make you stand in peace when you feel like you are crumbling and unleashing your lack of peace. He can meet you in that vulnerable place and supernaturally help you:

- Smile when you feel like frowning
- Laugh when you feel like crying
- Rejoice when you feel like mourning

The Spirit of the Lord is upon you! In your journaling today, write down the things that hinder you from being pleasant. What circumstances steal your peace and propel you toward a frustrated and irritated mama presence? What things can you do to help prevent yourself from setting a negative tone in your home?

"The Spirit of the LORD GOD is upon me,
because the LORD has anointed me to bring good news to the poor;
he has sent me to bind up the brokenhearted,
to proclaim liberty to the captives,
and the opening of the prison to those who are bound;
to proclaim the year of the LORD's favor,
and the day of vengeance of our God; to comfort all who mourn."
—Isaiah 61:1–2

Journal Notes

Day 3—Misplaced Mothering

"And he answered, 'You shall love the Lord your God with all your heart and with all your soul and with all your strength and with all your mind, and your neighbor as yourself.'"
—Luke 10:27

Coffee is great, but it's not where our strength comes from. Go to the Bread of Life this morning, Mama! Feeling weary? Go to Him. He does not grow faint or weary, but He understands your weariness and can help. Find Him in His Word and eat from His banquet table! When people feast on man's words rather than God's Word, it's like eating crumbs when God has a Thanksgiving feast waiting for you!

Many times we are starving spiritually because we fill up on junk food or appetizers, such as Facebook, blogs, and phone calls with friends. Not that there's anything inherently wrong with any of these, but they may make us think we're full. This is only a delusion that will leave us hungry again soon. They don't provide lasting satisfaction. We have One who satisfies us fully. Only the Word of God can bring true satisfaction. Only the Bread of Life can fill our souls.

Christians are designed to seek spiritual comfort and satisfaction in Christ, the Living Water. Open your Bible. Read. Pray. Look for God to encourage you as only He can. Look for strength in Him alone. Listen to the Bible. Hear. Enjoy. Meditate on it day and night and find a satisfaction this world will never know!

In your journaling today, write down the different ways you deny the Lord as your main source of strength. Include the people and things that rob the Lord from being your first go-to. Maybe it's food, a friend, shopping, or even Facebook. Whatever the idols are in your life that keep you from turning to God in prayer and His Word, write them down and proactively read the Word and pray today instead of turning to these things or people for your strength.

"The LORD does not faint or grow weary…He gives power to the faint, and to him who has no might He increases strength. Even youths shall faint and be weary, and young men shall fall exhausted; but they who wait for the LORD shall renew their strength; they shall mount up with wings like eagles; they shall run and not be weary; they shall walk and not faint."
—Isaiah 40:28b–31

Journal Notes

_____

_____

_____

_____

_____

_____

_____

_____

_____

_____

_____

_____

_____

_____

_____

Day 4—Joyful Wife Mothering

"It is better to live in a desert land than with a quarrelsome and fretful woman."
—*Proverbs 21:19*

What kind of wife does your husband live with? Does he live with a woman who:

- Is at peace, is joyful, and chooses to trust God?
- Knows when to hold her tongue and let the Holy Spirit work?
- Looks for ways to build communication bridges rather than tear them down?
- Looks for the very best in her husband and recognizes he may not be the best guy but he's her best guy?

The world and Satan are doing a huge disservice to Christian women by encouraging them "to give their husband a piece of their mind." God desires for us to be gentle and submissive as we are learning more about our husbands and seeking to follow their lead. God desires for us to come to them with a humble heart when we disagree and accept that our husbands won't always do what we want.

May we look for ways to lighten our husband's load rather than make it heavier. May we make him look forward to coming home rather than dreading it. May we speak well of him to the children when he is present and away. May we be a source of joy and not sorrow in his life.

Why? Because we want to honor Christ; we recognize in being a joy-filled, life-giving wife we are doing so ultimately for Christ. Because we know that being the opposite of these things not only wrecks our husband's life but our own and the lives of our children! Joyful Wife Mothering is a blessing to all those around us.

Ultimately, we need the power of Christ to live this out! We need supernatural strength! This is yet another reason to be in the Word daily. Listening to it. Reading it. Meditating on it. We need to be praising Him through song and running to Him in prayer as the hours go by.

When we abide in Him joy flows more naturally. Write down in your journal 3 areas you want to work in in your marriage. Also write out a prayer to your Father asking for His help! He wants to help you.

*"An excellent wife is the crown of her husband,
but she who brings shame is like rottenness in his bones."*
—*Proverbs 12:4*

Journal Notes

Day 5—Creative Quiet Time Mothering

"But when you pray, go into your room and shut the door and pray to your Father who is in secret. And your Father who sees in secret will reward you."
—Matthew 6:6

Quiet time. Where did that phrase come from? Not the Bible! We know Jesus went away to be by Himself, but we mamas rarely have that option, do we?

Normally when mamas are thinking of "quiet time," they picture sitting in their favorite chair with their Bible, notebook, pen in hand, and a hot cup of creamy coffee by their side. No noise. No distractions. Just them and the Lord.

But let's be honest, that's not always realistic if you're a mama (especially of little ones like me). Sure, sometimes it is, but not all the time. I know some mamas go to greater lengths to make it happen (setting their alarm and waking before everyone else). But you don't HAVE to. Don't bind yourself to quiet time legalism. Don't make quiet time an idol.

Here are practical ways to get in the Word as a busy mama:

- After the kids go to bed at night. I mean, why does it have to be in the morning?!
- Throughout the day as time allows WITH the children running around in the midst of chaos. Because chaos is a big part of life now, right?
- During the kid's naptime/quiet time. I homeschool, so my kids are always around. That means naptime is a perfect time to read.
- LISTEN to the Bible online. Keep it going throughout the day. I even leave it on when I exit the room. His Word does not return void, and I know it's going in my heart through my ears and into my little one's hearts as well.
- Reading the Word WITH my kids. In fact, teaching the Word is one of the very best ways to get His Word into our hearts.

Quiet time isn't always quiet...it hardly ever is! And that's ok! In your journaling today, write down three creative ways YOU will seek to get your "quiet time" in.

"So faith comes from hearing, and hearing through the word of Christ."
—Romans 10:17

Journal Notes

Day 6—Persistent Mothering

"And let us not grow weary of doing good,
for in due season we will reap, if we do not give up."
—*Galatians 6:9*

As I write this, I can tell you I had a hard, tear-filled morning. I kept thinking of the verse above. It greatly encouraged me. I reminded myself that as a mama I can grow weary in doing good, but "in due season, I will reap, IF I do not give up." I wanted to give up this morning. I had to go to my room three separate times to cry.

Do you ever have days like that and feel like giving up? The Lord knows. He knows how hard it is to be a mom and He says: "don't grow weary, don't give up." I toughened up, left my room, and walked out to the dining room table where the kids were eating breakfast and proceeded to finish our Bible study. We were studying Romans 12:9, which says "Let love be genuine. Abhor what is evil; hold fast to what is good." Yes, Lord! Hold fast to what is good! To hold fast to something means to remain "tightly secured" Remain tightly secured to what is good, mama.

It is GOOD for you to teach your children in the ways of the Lord; it is GOOD for you to serve your family, and it is GOOD for you to look for ways to bless your husband. Remain tightly secured to these things even in the midst of turmoil and tears. Don't grow weary in doing all this good, and remember in due season, you will reap if you do not give up!

There is so much to lose when we choose to give up, which is one reason we shouldn't see that as an option. We should see motherhood as a job we can't quit. Rather than throwing in the towel, pray for God to give you wisdom so you know what you can do to improve the situation. James 1:5 says, "If any of you lacks wisdom, let him ask God, who gives generously to all without reproach, and it will be given him."

In your journaling today, write down what you can say to yourself when you feel like giving up. What habit have you established when you feel like giving up? Running away? Losing your temper? What new habit can you establish now with the Lord's help?

"Those who sow in tears shall reap with shouts of joy!"
—*Psalm 126:5*

Journal Notes

_____

_____

_____

_____

_____

_____

_____

_____

_____

_____

_____

_____

_____

_____

Day 7—Trusting God Mothering

"It is better to take refuge in the LORD than to trust in man."
—*Psalm 118:8*

When we trust in man or ourselves, it is as if we are trying to find refuge in them. But there is only One we are to find refuge in, and that is in God Himself. Whoever we seek to put our trust in is the same one we are seeking to find refuge in. How silly of us to seek refuge in ourselves or others. It is a vain task. Only God can be our place of refuge.

Psalm 146:3 says, "Put not your trust in princes, in a son of man, in whom there is no salvation." It's as if God is saying, "These people cannot provide salvation as I can. Why in the world would they seek to trust man instead of Me?" Our mighty God is infinitely more powerful than the finite humans around us. His wisdom and understanding are way beyond our comprehension.

Don't put your trust in your parents—respect them and honor them—but don't make them your god. Wives, don't put your faith in your husband. He's a sinner just as you are. Don't expect him to fulfill God's role in your life.

Isaiah 36:6 says, "Behold, you are trusting in Egypt, that broken reed of a staff, which will pierce the hand of any man who leans on it. Such is Pharaoh king of Egypt to all who trust in him." I love that description of Egypt, a broken reed. This is what every man and nation is in comparison to God, and yet we continue to lean on them, and as God says, we are pierced because of it! We may see others as mighty oaks, but God sees them as not only a wimpy reed but also a crushed wimpy reed. He knows no man is worthy of our trust.

In your journaling today, write down ways you have been trusting in man. How have you been let down by this? Cling to the Lord TODAY, and find perfect refuge in Him!

"God is our refuge and strength, a very present help in trouble."
—*Psalm 46:1*

Journal Notes

Day 8—Renewed Mind Mothering

"Finally, brothers, whatever is true, whatever is honorable, whatever is just, whatever is pure, whatever is lovely, whatever is commendable, if there is any excellence, if there is anything worthy of praise, think about these things."
—Philippians 4:8

Perspective is everything. If two women live out the same situations and circumstances, but one is depressed and the other is joyful, the difference is their perspectives. Our perspectives are directly related to what we think.

What do you think about often? If we had a live recording of your thoughts, would they be on what is true? Honorable? Just? Pure? Lovely? Commendable? I know I have some stinking thinking going on way too often and our stinking thinking impacts not only us but also our children and husbands! They suffer at the hand of us disobeying Philippians 4:8, and that's what it really is, disobedience.

God didn't say if you feel like it, or if everything is going your way, think on all this good stuff. He simply commanded you to "think about these things." The good news is it gets easier the more often you do it. When you intentionally change your perspective to think on whatever is true, honorable, just, pure, lovely, commendable, excellent, and worthy of praise; then it becomes more natural. The more you choose self-pity and think on whatever is untrue, not honorable, unjust, impure, unlovely, not commendable, not excellent, and unworthy of praise; the more natural that will become.

Pay special attention to your thoughts today and watch how they impact your perspective! In fact, carry your devotional around, and in the journal section write down word for word all negative thoughts you have so you can SEE them. After you write your thought, list a Bible verse that directly speaks against your thought.

When you start to go down a bad trail in your mind, choose instead to think on Philippians 4:8!

"Do not be conformed to this world, but be transformed by the renewal of your mind, that by testing you may discern what is the will of God, what is good and acceptable and perfect."
—Romans 12:2

Journal Notes

Day 9—Peace-pursuing Mothering

"So then let us pursue what makes for peace and for mutual upbuilding."
—Romans 14:19

Pursue the things which make for peace. Oh, that I would set a good example of this for my children to follow so that they would understand what it means to pursue peace with one another!

The Greek word here for pursue is *diōkō*, and it means: "To run swiftly in order to catch a person or thing, to run after, to seek after eagerly, earnestly endeavor to acquire."[i]

That's good. That's hard.

Do you RUN after peace? Do you earnestly endeavor to edify those around you? And by "around you," I mean within the four walls of your home.

Christ pursued us. He earnestly endeavored for you and me to have peace between ourselves and our Father. Christ edifies us daily.

Because of His pursuit, we should want to pursue. Because of His edifying, we should want to edify. We should be running after peace in our relationships with our family members. Is this the case in your relationship with your children? Do you struggle more experiencing peace with one child than another? Seek the Lord and ask Him how He would have you lead the way in peace with your children. The Lord wants you to have peace in your home so you can trust He will answer your prayers in this area if you will allow Him to lead and convict you.

For your journaling activity today, come back to your devotional and write down each time you were tempted to run AWAY from peace with your children and/or husband. Pay special attention to these times in the future because you know they are particularly difficult for you to pursue peace in! Seek to put off strife and anger in these moments and to put on peace and joy.

"If possible, so far as it depends on you, live peaceably with all."
—Romans 12:18

Journal Notes

Day 10—Consistent and Content Mothering

"Whoever spares the rod hates his son,
but he who loves him is diligent to discipline him."
—*Proverbs 13:24*

What kind of mama are you by nature? Are you the type who wants to give in, allows your kids to lead, and struggles with consistency? OR Are you the mama who loves structure, strives to be consistent in discipline, and has no problem telling your kids no?

Well, unfortunately, I can relate to the first type of mama more. That's why this quote by Sally Clarkson really resonates with me:

When we give our children every single thing they want and meet every single need, we're actually giving them idols. We're causing them to be spoiled. We're making them think they deserve for the whole world to come and bow at their feet, and provide everything they want.

Sometimes we feel like our kids need to be happy all the time and have so many things ... Parents don't realize they are hindering their children by giving them the illusion that having things and having experiences is a right, and is something that's actually going to make them happy ... actually, having more makes you more discontent.[ii]

Persevere mama—for His name's sake and glory. And don't forget, no matter what kind of mama you are, teach your children this isn't our home and we need very little to be content!

In your journaling today, write down three areas you are lacking contentment in. For each one, write a corresponding reason to be thankful. Also, write down what kind of mama you are. The one who always gives in, or the one who always stands firm. Maybe you are too stern, and the children often feel like they are soldiers more than your children or maybe they feel more like your little buddy you are continually giving in to. Ask the Lord how you can specifically grow as a mama in this regard!

"But if we have food and clothing, with these we will be content."
—*1 Timothy 6:8*

Journal Notes

Day 11—Doing What You Can Mothering

*"Jesus answered him, 'Truly, truly, I say to you,
unless one is born again he cannot see the kingdom of God.'"*
—John 3:3

My husband prays EVERY night for our children's salvation. Is there really anything more important for us to pray as parents? I don't think so!

But what can we NOT do?

- We can't save them. We can't reach into their hearts and cram the gospel in there and make it grow.
- We can't homeschool them as a guarantee they will receive Christ and follow Him faithfully. (Look at Cain and Abel. The first homeschooled children…one followed faithfully, and one brutally murdered his brother).
- We can't force them into the Kingdom of God. We can't coerce them or beg them to be born again. We can't make promises that if they say the sinner's prayer they will never have to fear hell. We can't create genuine conviction and repentance in the hearts of our children.

What can we do?

- We can pray with and for them.
- We can be transparent with them and authentic in our faith sharing our own failings and weaknesses.
- We can share the gospel with them over and over and over.
- We can faithfully open the Word of God with them every day teaching them and instructing them.

We can and should do a lot of things. But we can't save our children. In your journaling today, write down three things you can do with and for your children and three things you can't. Also, write down three ways you can be authentic in your faith with your children.

"For by grace you have been saved through faith. And this is not your own doing; it is the gift of God, not a result of works, so that no one may boast."
—Ephesians 2:8–9

Journal Notes

Day 12—Kind Mothering

"Put on then, as God's chosen ones, holy and beloved,
compassionate hearts, kindness, humility, meekness, and patience."
—Colossians 3:12

George Swinnock wrote, "Reprove compassionately. Soft words and hard arguments do well together. Passion will heat the sinner's blood, but compassion will heal his conscience."[iii] This is a great quote for us to remember as mamas and wives! Maybe we should have this in every room of our home!

As mamas, we have a lot of reproving and correcting to do, don't we? A lot of our days are filled with such things. But HOW we reprove, train, and discipline matters very much.

There is just something about a gentle person who impacts those around them to be gentler, and there is just something about an aggressive, angry person who causes those around them to be more aggressive and angry. "Make no friendship with a man given to anger, nor go with a wrathful man, lest you learn his ways and entangle yourself in a snare" (Proverbs 22:24–25).

We must live out what we want to see in our children—even when it feels like our blood is boiling!

When you feel that angry jolt in your spirit, recognize it, and put on compassion and gentleness instead. Say a kind, intentional word rather than a rash, hurtful one. Replace your childish responses to adult-like, mature ones! Ask the Lord to help and guide you in this area. He wants to be there with you in this difficult task. The Spirit is your Helper! Ask Him to help you!

In your journaling today, I want you to answer these questions: If you were in a new job, how would you want the person training you to speak to you? What if you kept fumbling up every task or forgetting what your trainer had said? How would you want them to respond?

Remember, our children have been here on earth for a much shorter time than us. Let's show them the grace, compassion, kindness, and patience we would desire when at a new place.

"A soft answer turns away wrath..."
—Proverbs 15:1

Journal Notes

_____

_____

_____

_____

_____

_____

_____

_____

_____

_____

_____

_____

_____

_____

Day 13—Servant Mothering

"And Mary said, 'Behold, I am the servant of the Lord;
let it be to me according to your word.'"
—Luke 1:38

What a beautiful response Mary gives in this verse to the angel Gabriel who gave her some VERY hard news to hear. What hard spots does the Lord have in your life right now? Do you have a willing and moldable heart like Mary? Are you able to say: "Behold, I am the servant of the Lord; let it be to me according to your word."?

Here's the good news. The Lord doesn't expect this of us, but He expects this of Christ in us. If we surrender to Christ and are in His Word daily, He is better able to work through and strengthen and empower us to live a life of submission and joy intertwined.

A mother's life is a servant's life. There is no way around that. The sooner we embrace it, as Mary did, the sooner we will ENJOY motherhood. The more we resist it, the more we will disdain our calling. When we say to the Lord: "Let it be to me according to Your Word," it's as if we are saying: "Do with me as you please, Lord. Use me up as Your vessel. Work through me as You desire not as my flesh desires."

What does your flesh desire? Write a list on the journaling page.

Did you write it out? Now look at that list. You will find nothing good or of eternal worth.

Now, write down what your spirit desires in mothering. Now, look at that list.

That is a beautiful list! When we seek the things of the Spirit and not the things of the flesh, we are like Mary saying: "Behold, I am your servant, do with me as you please Lord. I am Yours."

"The greatest among you shall be your servant. Whoever exalts himself will be
humbled, and whoever humbles himself will be exalted."
—Matthew 23:11–12

Journal Notes

Day 14—Faithful Marriage Mothering

"An excellent wife who can find? She is far more precious than jewels."
—Proverbs 31:10

Christian women hear five common lies about marriage. They can lead to divorce and/or misery:

Lie #1: "If he doesn't make you happy, you shouldn't be with him. God wants you to be happy." Where is the Scripture that says: "God wants you to be happy"? God wants you to be holy. God wants you to be committed. God wants your yes to be yes, your "I do" to be your "I do." He wants your life, including your marriage, to bring Him glory. Marriage, like everything else in your life, is about Him and for Him.

Lie #2: "You married too young." ??? What does that even mean? Is there an age we reach where we stop changing? Whether you marry at age eighteen or age forty, you did not marry too young or too old. We all change and grow, regardless of what age we marry. Change is not a means for divorce.

Lie #3: "I'd be happier with someone else." Maybe that would be true. But why? Because that person will give you what you want? That's not what the Christian life is about either. Most likely though, it's not true. Every person is an annoying sinner with all their unique, difficult sins that God can use to make you more dependent on Him.

Lie #4: "I married the wrong person." If you're married, then you're married to the right person.

Lie #5: "We're incompatible." Every person on the planet is incompatible for another person because no two people are the same. The questions are: "What will you do with the incompatibility? How will you seek to adapt to your husband to make your incompatibility less of a strain on your marriage?"

Don't listen to these lies. God designed marriage to be for life. I understand you may be hurting and there may be some SERIOUS issues in your marriage. If that's the case, don't quit, get biblical help. In your journaling today, write down which lie or lies you tend to gravitate toward and then write down why they are lies for you. Write down truths next to the lies.

"'... and the two shall become one flesh.' So they are no longer two but one flesh. What therefore God has joined together, let not man separate.'"
—Mark 10:8–9

Journal Notes

Day 15—New Creation Mothering

"Remember not the former things, nor consider the things of old.
Behold, I am doing a new thing; now it springs forth, do you not perceive it?
I will make a way in the wilderness and rivers in the desert."
—Isaiah 43:18–19

How we start our day is so important. Doing this devotional in the morning is a great way to begin our day with our hearts and minds set on Him and things above, not on things of the earth.

Here is one eternal reminder for you today: if you are in Christ, you ARE a new creation. The old has passed away! Behold! The new HAS come. This can be a real struggle for some mamas to embrace. Maybe you often don't feel like you have been made new. Maybe it feels like the old is still around. That is because the flesh is still present. Romans 7 makes that clear. But at the same time, God says those in Christ are a new creation!

Picture a butterfly moping around all day because she still feels like a caterpillar. Imagine all her butterfly friends encouraging her to remember she is a new creation, the old has passed away, and she is no longer a caterpillar and never will be again! But this butterfly just won't believe it, and so she spends the rest of her potential filled butterfly life miserable thinking she is still a caterpillar. That's us when we refuse to believe what God has said!

We don't get to decide who or what we are. He does, and He says we ARE a new creation. Give thanks to your Father for the good work He has done in you and cling to the promise you are a new creation in Him.

In your journaling today, write down ways you don't feel like a creation. Look at the list and pray about how you can change to become more like that new creation you long for!

"Therefore, if anyone is in Christ, he is a new creation.
The old has passed away; behold, the new has come."
—2 Corinthians 5:17

Journal Notes

Day 16—Abiding in Christ Mothering

"Abide in Me, and I in you. As the branch cannot bear fruit by itself, unless it abides in the vine, neither can you, unless you abide in Me."
—*John 15:4*

Are you feeling like a failure? I am. I constantly fail as a wife, a mother, and a Christian. These words from Tozer blessed my socks off! I pray they do the same for you. A.W. Tozer said:

> In this world, men [and women] are judged by their ability to do. They are rated according to the distance they have come up the hill of achievement. At the bottom is utter failure; at the top complete success, and between these two extremes the majority of civilized men sweat and struggle from youth to old age. But in all of this, there is no happiness. The effort to succeed puts too much strain on the nerves. The man who reaches the pinnacle is seldom happy for very long. The mania to succeed is a GOOD THING PERVERTED. The desire to fulfill the purpose for which we were created is, of course, a gift from God, but sin has twisted this impulse about and turned it into a selfish lust for first place.[iv]

Much of our failure in succeeding is because we seek our glory, honor, and praise. When we do all for His glory and His sake, we find supernatural joy and help in our pursuits. We also often grow weary because we are pursuing more than the Lord would have for us. One practical way to not be so overwhelmed in doing too much is to seek your husband's counsel. Ask him what he thinks are the top five things he thinks you should be investing your time and energy in. This has helped me so much in deciphering what is best for me to pursue and not pursue. It also helps clarify WHY I am doing certain things.

Pray! Seek Him and then write in the journaling section areas in your life that distract you from seeking to succeed for the Lord's sake and not your own.

"In the same way, let your light shine before others, so that they may see your good works and GIVE GLORY TO YOUR FATHER WHO IS IN HEAVEN."
—*Matthew 5:16*

Journal Notes

_____

_____

_____

_____

_____

_____

_____

_____

_____

_____

_____

_____

_____

Day 17—Equipped Mothering

*"Teach me Your way, O LORD, that I may walk in Your truth;
unite my heart to fear Your name."*
—Psalm 86:11

In our internet-drenched society, it can be tempting as a mama to think:

- "I just need to read ONE more article on discipline to get it right."
- "I bet if I find that perfect podcast, I will have the answer to a better marriage."
- "I just need to go to Pinterest and find another pin that will help me be a better homemaker."

In reality, mamas, we waste a lot of time "researching" and reading only to feel more overwhelmed than we did before. King Solomon said, "Of making many books there is no end, and much study is a weariness of the flesh" (Ecclesiastes 12:12b). How true this can be in our day of endless blogs and podcasts!

We would probably do ourselves a lot of good to set our phones down, close our laptops, and read to our children or sing a few songs with them. How about loving on our husbands when we don't feel like it? Maybe we should get up and do the dishes and laundry.

We should do what we already know is right at the very moment we feel convicted to do it.

Go get 'em, Mama! You are equipped better than you know, and if you don't feel that way, run to the Equipper! We should go to the perfect Word more and to the imperfect internet less.

In your journaling today, write down ten mama truths you already know and just need to walk in! Refrain from searching for something new and just live out the truth already revealed to you.

"His divine power has granted to us all things that pertain to life and godliness, through the knowledge of Him who called us to His own glory and excellence."
—2 Peter 1:3

Journal Notes

Day 18—Small Things Mothering

*"Then the word of the LORD came to me, saying,
'The hands of Zerubbabel have laid the foundation of this house; his hands shall also complete it. Then you will know that the LORD of hosts has sent me to you. For whoever has despised the day of small things shall rejoice, and shall see the plumb line in the hand of Zerubbabel'"*
—Zechariah 4:8–10

Have you heard this verse before? God says, "Do not despise the day of small things." I love this, especially since I'm a stay-at-home mom! Sometimes it seems like each day is filled only with small things. My love for the verse made me want to study it and what I discovered increased my affection for it!

The Lord was encouraging Zerubbabel through the prophet Zechariah by letting him know that not only has he laid the foundation for the temple, but the Lord will also use Zerubbabel to complete it! And what would he complete? Something magnificent! The temple from which people would worship the Almighty!

Even the beginning of great things like building the temple for the Lord can be despised! God has called us mamas to build a mighty thing: a home. A home in which our children come to:

- Know the Lord and His teachings
- Learn what it means to worship Him daily
- Understand marriage, hard work, and character

We are laying a mighty foundation in our homes daily even though we may seem to fill our days with "small things."

Moses wrote, "Let the favor of the Lord our God be upon us, and establish the work of our hands upon us; yes, establish the work of our hands" (Psalm 90:17). This should be our prayer too! In your journaling today, consider what is it that makes us despise the day of small things. Pride? A sense that we are "above it"? Do you enjoy small things? Write down your thoughts and search your heart and pray for the Lord to give you a heart for even the smallest of things today.

"Whatever you do, work heartily, as for the Lord and not for men, knowing that from the Lord you will receive the inheritance as your reward. You are serving the Lord Christ."
—Colossians 3:23–24

Journal Notes

Day 19—Submissive Wife Mothering

"Children, obey your parents in the Lord, because this is right.
'Honor your father and mother' (this is the first commandment with a promise),
'that it may go well with you and that you may live long in the land.'"
—Ephesians 6:1–3

The Greek word for obey in the verse above is *hypakouō*. It means: "To listen, to harken to a command, to be obedient to, submit to."v That sounds nice, doesn't it?! Children who listen! Children who harken to our commands for them as if it were their duty!

Paul gives a similar verse to wives in relation to their husbands. First Peter 3:1 tells us, "Likewise, wives, be subject to your own husbands, so that even if some do not obey the word, they may be won without a word by the conduct of their wives…" That phrase "be subject to…" is *hypotassō* in the Greek.vi Very similar to the Greek word for the command given to children to obey their parents, isn't it?! *Hypotassō* means: to arrange under, to subordinate, put in subjection, to subject one's self, obey, to submit to one's control, to yield to one's admonition or advice."

Remember when I asked you how nice it sounds to have children who obey us like the Word commands? I am thinking it sounds just as nice to husbands to have wives who arrange themselves under, obey them, and yield to them.

Maybe you are thinking, "What? Why does she keep talking about being a wife? This is supposed to be about mothering!" I keep talking about this because what you are as a wife directly impacts what you are as a mother!

Be extra aware today of how you feel when your children disobey you or have a bad attitude toward you, and then imagine your husband feeling that way when you are unsubmissive toward him. Seek to joyfully put yourself under him as you want your children to obey you joyfully.

Journal which areas you are most tempted to not submit to your husband in and then write down how you will overcome these temptations with the Spirit's help.

"Now as the church submits to Christ,
so also wives should submit in everything to their husbands."
—Ephesians 5:24

Journal Notes

Day 20—Thoughtful Words Mothering

"Love is patient and kind; love does not envy or boast; it is not arrogant or rude. It does not insist on its own way; it is not irritable or resentful."
—1 Corinthians 13:4–5

Any other mamas out there struggle with their tempers? Oh, I hate it. I hate how I let my flesh win: "The evil I will not to do, that I practice" (Romans 7:19b).

I was so encouraged reading Ephesians 4:29: "Let no corrupting talk come out of your mouths, but only such as is good for building up, as fits the occasion, that it may give grace to those who hear."

What a great mama verse! Are we setting an example for our children in how we speak to them in less than ideal circumstances? Are we quick to lash out letting corrupting talk flow from our mouths?

The Greek word here for corrupting means: rotten.[vii] It is the same Greek word used over and over in the gospels when describing bad fruit. In other words, our mouths are spewing forth bad, rotten fruit when we yell at our children or say harsh things to them.

Here's another excellent verse on this topic: "A word fitly spoken is like apples of gold in a setting of silver" (Proverbs 25:11).

In other words, when we speak good, timely words to our children, it is a BEAUTIFUL thing. God sees our speech toward our children as having the potential to be attractive/appealing or rotting/detrimental.

May our Father help us today to speak what is good to our children, building them up and giving them grace with our words. May we speak to them in a way that turns them toward not only God but also toward us and not away from us.

Carry your devotional with you today and write down words you are tempted to say to your children but you know you shouldn't. Write those in a column you title: "Put off." Have another column that says: "Put on." For everything you say in the put off column write next to it in the put on column something godly and helpful to say. What are some common hurtful/non-helpful things you say to your children? What are some things you can say in place of those?

"Through Him then let us continually offer up a sacrifice of praise to God, that is, the fruit of lips that acknowledge His name."
—Hebrews 13:15

Journal Notes

Day 21—Empathetic Mothering

*"Let each of you look not only to his own interests,
but also to the interests of others."*
—Philippians 2:4

If you are anything like me, you can sometimes forget your children are little humans. They are like us, just younger versions. They are fallen image-bearers as we are. They desire empathy, understanding, grace, love, patience, and encouragement just as much, if not more than we do.

How do you want others to treat you when you are sad? How do you want to be encouraged when feeling defeated? What gracious reply do you need when you mess up… again? Our children want the same.

I'll give you a practical example with my son. He worked hard on a drawing and his little sister colored all over it. His eyes filled with tears, and he was frustrated. The old Katie would have responded with something like: "It's just a piece of paper, you can draw another one." But when I tried to put myself in his place and imagine I had worked hard on something only for someone to come along and trash it, my response was: "I'm sorry, Honey! That is hard when you work on something only for someone to destroy it. But you still need to forgive your little sister. Let's think of something else you can draw, and try to put it up high when you finish so she can't reach it."

Empathy. Grace. Helpful direction. Those are things we need, and those are things our children need. Impatience, lashing out, and barking at our children are not helpful and are definitely not ways we wish for others to treat us.

Write down five ways you like others to treat you when you are going through a hard time. Seek to treat your children in that way when they are going through something tough. Pray and ask the Lord to give you eyes to see your children as little people who wish to be treated the same way you want to be.

"And as you wish that others would do to you, do so to them."
—Luke 6:31

Journal Notes

Day 22—Quiet Life Mothering

"Aspire to live quietly, and to mind your own affairs,
and to work with your hands, as we instructed you."
—*1 Thessalonians 4:11*

This has become one of my life verses. As women, we can get caught up in all sorts of affairs that are not ours to worry about. Know what I mean? Facebook, the news, and gossip do not help. I love that in some translations, this reads: "Make it your ambition to lead a quiet life…" A quiet life. Hmmm… does that sound like your life? Minding your own affairs?

The world tempts us to make it our ambition to make a name for ourselves, do something grand, have a perfect-looking Pinterest home, be up-to-date on all the latest fashions, or have the ideal body. All those are vain, but something as simple as living a quiet life and minding our own business is a great thing to aspire to!

In school, I remember my teacher often saying: "Keep your eyes on your own page." Some of us mamas need to be doing more of this. We need to be minding our own affairs and keeping our eyes on our page. The Lord has given us plenty to do. We don't need to worry about what others are or are not doing.

The next part of the verse continues with its simple, perfect instruction: "work with your hands." Talk about basic and yet so lacking in our culture. We can be lazy as keepers of the home. We despise working with our hands, when we should be making our homes into clean havens. We can be tempted to consider texting as a form of "working with our hands." God desires for us mamas to be busy about His work for our lives which includes lots of working with our hands. Embrace that work today!

What distracts you from minding your affairs and working with your hands? Write those things down and pray and ask the Lord how you can better live out this verse.

"But seek first the kingdom of God and His righteousness,
and all these things will be added to you."
—*Matthew 6:33*

Journal Notes

Day 23—Good Attitude Mothering

*"You hypocrites! Well did Isaiah prophesy of you, when he said:
'This people honors Me with their lips, but their heart is far from Me'"*
—Matthew 15:7–8

Our attitude as the mama is very contagious. How we act impacts our home terribly, or wonderfully.

If your children and husband answered honestly what would they say your attitude is like most of the time? How about when you are enduring less than ideal circumstances? Are you irritable? Grumpy? On edge? Lacking joy?

We cannot harp on our children for their bad attitudes if we are constantly displaying a bad attitude ourselves. That's called hypocritical parenting, and nothing can poison our relationship with our children faster!

Listen to this powerful verse from Paul on hypocrisy and see how it applies to parenting! "You then who teach others, do you not teach yourself?" (Romans 2:21).

This has become one of my all-time favorite go-to parenting verses. I feel like the Spirit regularly brings it to mind when my expectations for my children exceed my expectations for myself. This is an area we have to be on constant high alert if we don't want to have bitter adult children

Be prayerful about the ways you may be having a stinky attitude but especially be prayerful about the ways you are teaching your children things you really are not willing to teach or live out yourself! Let's pray who we are at home is who we are at church. Nothing drives children away from the church faster than parents who are one person on Sunday morning and a different person the rest of the week.

In the journal section for today, write down three areas you are hypocritical in your parenting and pray for the Lord to help you repent of the hypocrisy! Maybe even plan on talking to your children and asking them to forgive you for not teaching yourself what you are teaching them.

*"Show yourself in all respects to be a model of good works,
and in your teaching show integrity [and] dignity."*
—Titus 2:7

Journal Notes

Day 24—Prayerful Mothering

"Gladden the soul of Your servant, for to You, O Lord, do I lift up my soul.
For You, O Lord, are good and forgiving, abounding in steadfast love to all who call
upon You. Give ear, O LORD, to my prayer; listen to my plea for grace.
In the day of my trouble I call upon You, for You answer me."
—*Psalm 86:4–7*

Oh, what a BEAUTIFUL prayer! Prayer is tough sometimes, isn't it? It's hard to know what to pray, but we can be encouraged that we can always pray the prayers in Scripture!

When we see the Lord as a gracious and loving Master, it is easier to lift up our souls to Him. He is a good and forgiving God, abounding in steadfast love for you, Mama! He is worthy of your prayers and listens to your pleas for grace, and we need lots of grace, don't we? Grace for us is like gasoline for a car. Grace is what fuels us to get through our days. As we pray for grace from our Master and it fills us, we can then have it overflow onto our children throughout the day.

We experience a different kind of trouble daily than David did. The Hebrew word for trouble in this passage is *tsarah,* and it means "adversity, affliction, anguish, distress."[viii] I would say that can describe different parts of our days as mamas, wouldn't you? The sibling rivalries, the heartache from our sin, the constant physical and emotional demands. We have much *"tsarah"* we can bring to the Lord and trust He will answer us.

Do you automatically call upon the Lord in your moments of trouble? Do you see Him as the forgiving Master who can help you and who hears you? As you go throughout your day and experience different forms of "mama *tsarah*," write in your journal what is happening in your heart and then call upon God as David does here in Psalm 86. Also, write out Psalm 86:4–7 in your journal page and say it out loud to the Lord as your prayer.

"Oh give thanks to the LORD; call upon His name;
make known His deeds among the peoples!"
—*1 Chronicles 16:8*

Journal Notes

Day 25—Rejoicing Mothering

"Rejoice in the Lord always; again I will say, rejoice.
Let your reasonableness be known to everyone."
—*Philippians 4:4–5a*

These verses are familiar, aren't they? There are so many familiar verses that I fail to live out as a mama. Rejoice always, Lord? Oh! But look what it says: "in the Lord." These are key words. It would be one thing if the command were simply to rejoice, but it is a whole other thing to rejoice IN THE LORD.

We are called to rejoice in our Lord, by our Lord, and with our Lord. We are not alone in this large task of rejoicing always! He can help us. When we don't feel like rejoicing, we can hide in Him and find a way because He is good; He is worthy of our rejoicing regardless of our circumstances that make it difficult to rejoice.

With that in mind, the Lord then exhorts us to let our reasonableness be known to everyone. The word for reasonableness means: "appropriate, fitting, becoming, fair, mild, gentle."[ix] This can seem like an impossible endeavor—especially when we are called to live this way in our home! BUT when we are hiding in the Lord and rejoicing in Him, we naturally live in a becoming, fair, mild and gentle way, don't we? It's when we forget who we are in Him that we act in inappropriate, unreasonable, and harsh ways.

As eternally minded mamas, we must seek to rejoice not in our circumstances—or we will fall over and over—but when we seek to rejoice in Him, we will have a continual reason to celebrate. Show your children today what it means to rejoice in the Lord.

What makes you rejoice? Write it down on your journaling page. List what you think of when you hear the word rejoice. Write down practical ways you will choose to rejoice today.

"Walk in a manner worthy of the Lord, fully pleasing to Him: bearing fruit in every
good work and increasing in the knowledge of God; being strengthened with all
power, according to His glorious might, for all endurance and patience with joy"
—*Colossians 1:10–11*

Journal Notes

Day 26—God-approved Mothering

"For am I now seeking the approval of man, or of God? Or am I trying to please man? If I were still trying to please man, I would not be at servant of Christ."
—Galatians 1:10

These are great verses for us to ask every day. "Am I now seeking the approval of man, or of God? Am I trying to please man?" When we seek to please man, we are no longer living as a servant of Christ.

We can fall into wanting to please man as a mama, too. It's easy to do. It may look different for different mamas. Some mamas may want to impress man with the way their homes look. They don't keep the home because they want to honor Christ, they keep the home because they want to please man. Some mamas may go to great measures to make sure their children behave in public not because they want to be a good reflection of Christ, but because they want the approval and praise of man. We are not fooling God when we are seeking the approval of man, mamas. He knows our hearts and sees our intentions.

Even though Paul directed these next verses to bondservants, we can still apply them since we are bondservants for Christ! "Bondservants, obey your earthly masters with fear and trembling, with a sincere heart, as you would Christ, not by the way of eye-service, as people-pleasers, but as bondservants of Christ, doing the will of God from the heart, rendering service with a good will as to the Lord and not to man, knowing that whatever good anyone does, this he will receive back from the Lord, whether he is a bondservant or is free" (Ephesians 6:5–8). We mamas must live this life with a sincere heart not by way of eye-service, but as bondservants of Christ, willing to do the will of God from our hearts, rendering service in our homes as if it were all unto the Lord. We can celebrate that when we serve for the Lord and not for man that we will receive back from the Lord. We work for the Lord, mamas! He is our Employer!

What would your day look like if you envisioned the Lord's eyes fixed on you in your home instead of living out eye-service for man? Record on your journal page what comes to mind when answering this question.

"So whether we are at home or away, we make it our aim to please Him."
—2 Corinthians 5:9

Journal Notes

Day 27—Focused Mothering

"Behold, children are a heritage from the LORD, the fruit of the womb a reward."
—*Psalm 127:3*

At the time of writing this, my seventh baby just turned five months old.

The other morning when she woke, even though I was tired, she brought a smile to my face when I saw her. She always does. As I walked into her room, she squealed out of happiness and wiggled all over. I unwrapped her out of her swaddling blanket like a gift from the Lord. That's what she is.

After that, I went into my room, and while I nursed her, I was reading organization articles on my phone, and I felt a prompting: "Why don't you hold her hand instead of your phone while you nurse her?"

I grabbed her tiny hand... I loved how she responded as she gripped my fingers tightly so as to say: "Love you, Mommy. Thank you for holding my hand." I started rubbing her little hand with my thumb and thanking God that unlike my phone, she was made by Him and sent to me.

Too often we are looking at our text messages when we should be looking at our kids. Too often we are holding our phone when we should be holding our children on our laps. Too often we are looking for our phone when we should be looking for our children so that we can spend more time with them. Too often we are listening for the text notifications when we should be listening to their cute little stories. And too often we are reading on our phones when we should be reading God's Word to us.

Eternally minded mamas don't live like other mamas.

Write down three practical ways you will engage with your children today!! It takes intention. We can become so tech-oriented that we lose sight of what matters.

May God help us!

"Train the young women to love their husbands and children."
—*Titus 2:4*

Journal Notes

Day 28—Faith-filled Mothering

"Now faith is the assurance of things hoped for,
the conviction of things not seen."
—Hebrews 11:1

Doubts are usually born out of what we see. Faith calls us to look to what is unseen. In Hebrews 11:1, we read a perfect definition of faith: "Now faith is the assurance of things hoped for, the conviction of things not seen." Did you catch that? It comprehends as fact what we CANNOT experience by the physical senses. In other words, true faith and trust in God are not found in our physical experiences.

When we look to what is seen and felt, we are setting ourselves up for doubt and running from trust in God. Everything we see was made out of what is unseen.

If I asked you "Do you have faith that God created the world?" You would say, "Of course, there is a Creator. I mean look around! How could this all just get here?!" Well, I would say to you, "that same faith and trust you have in God regarding creation is the faith He calls us to have in all areas of life. He is calling you to have faith in the unseen, not the seen just as you do when you look at the world around you and have faith that God created it and made it out of what is unseen. In that sense, you have perfect faith in the unseen."

It's easier for us to trust that God in His great power, wisdom, and goodness made the universe, but in that same power, wisdom, and goodness we don't trust Him to help us in our day to day lives or even in the tragedies we face.

When you look outside today at God's awesome creation, ask Him to give you faith that the same power He has to make everything from nothing is the same power He has to work in your daily life.

Write down three areas in your life that need more faith. Write out a prayer sharing with the Lord your lack of faith.

"I believe; help my unbelief!"
—Mark 9:24

Journal Notes

Day 29—Sanctified Mothering

"I have been crucified with Christ. It is no longer I who live, but Christ who lives in me. And the life I now live in the flesh I live by faith in the Son of God, who loved me and gave Himself for me."
—Galatians 2:20

We crave comfort more than sanctification. I don't know about you, but this one hits home for me. I love comfort and crave convenience. I want it my way, all day, every day in every way, and I start to lose trust in God when He seems more interested in my sanctification than my "comfortication."

When we have more interest in being comfortable than being like Christ, you better believe we will lose our trust in God. This is why when we are suffering, we often find ourselves doubting Him, His goodness, His love for us, and His plan for our lives. Instead of believing what Galatians 2:20 says, we believe: "I have not been crucified with Christ. I am alive and well and I want what I want when I want it, and the life I now live is in the flesh not by faith but by sight, feeling, emotion, desire, lusts, and cravings."

But when we crave sanctification MORE than "comfortication," our trust in God grows exponentially. One who craves comfort more than sanctification will never rejoice in their suffering. Their suffering becomes the microphone through which they shout in anger at God and question and doubt Him.

God has designed us to become more like His Son, and He has a lot of sanctifying to do to make us more like Christ. So the next time you are not trusting God in the midst of discomfort, see if you are craving comfort more than sanctification and then pray and ask God to give you a heart for sanctification more than comfort. I guarantee it will grow your faith.

In your journaling today name three areas in your life that you crave "comfortication" more than sanctification. Find three Bible verse to correspond with each area you have mentioned that will spur you on toward sanctification instead!

"Not only that, but we rejoice in our sufferings, knowing that suffering produces endurance, and endurance produces character, and character produces hope, and hope does not put us to shame."
—Romans 5:3–5a

Journal Notes

Day 30—Respectful Wife Mothering

"Wives, submit to your husbands, as is fitting in the Lord."
—Colossians 3:18

Expectations. We have a lot of them, don't we? The question is, where are they coming from? There are really only two places we should be concerned about them coming from—God and our husbands. That simplifies things, doesn't it?!

In Colossians 3:18, God calls us to submit to our husbands. Adapting and submitting are synonymous. We need to adapt to our husband's vision for our homes and make his vision a reality!

This has been a long process for me. I am still in the middle of it really. I am trying to ask my husband things like: "What would you like me to get done today?" "If I could only clean our room or the living area, which would you choose?" "Do you think (fill in the blank) is a good use of my time?" "Should I do this with so and so?" "Would you like me to do that for you?"

Asking these sorts of questions does not come naturally to me, but they are good and right questions. We should ask our husbands of their expectations of us and forget about others expectations (including those found on Pinterest). Only with prayer and intention is this possible.

Does this mean we have no say in how the home looks or what we do with our day? No. But we should be seeking our husband's desires above our own.

How about you? Does it come naturally for you to ask what your husband would like for you to do? Be sure to ask him today! When you ask your husband these sorts of things it practically demonstrates to him you respect him and his wishes. Write down his top three needs/requests in the journal section. Also, write down why this might be hard for your flesh. Start making his vision for your home a reality today.

"...let the wife see that she respects her husband."
—Ephesians 5:33

Journal Notes

Day 31—Eternally Minded Mothering

"Set your minds on things that are above, not on things that are on earth."
—Colossians 3:2

This verse is what inspired Eternally Minded Mamas. What does it mean to be eternally minded in our mothering?? It means keeping our hearts and minds set on things above in the midst of the temporal and mundane.

So much of mothering seems like getting up and doing the same thing over and over: changing diapers, working out sibling quarrels, doing dishes, making meals, cleaning up spills, organizing and decluttering.

Doesn't seem very exciting does it? But when we seek Christ in these daily tasks it can be thrilling because we know we are ultimately serving the King of kings Himself!

This isn't easy. This takes hourly intention and remembering. It's not easy but it's possible with Christ because He is the One commanding us in this verse to set our minds on things that are above and so we can trust that with His help we can be eternally minded in our mothering.

One last thing as you conclude your 31-day journey. You have so many eternal blessings in Christ that don't change regardless of how rough your day has been as a mama. Isn't that so encouraging?! Our eternal status remains the same!

In Christ we are adopted, redeemed, forgiven, saved, sealed, and given special insight into His will. What does He want in return? A life of slavery to good works? A life filled with self-affliction? A continual pattern of self-loathing to show Him we are really sorry? Nope. He just wants our praise and hearts.

Remember mama, let your eternal status squash your temporary circumstances. Read Ephesians 1:3-14 in your bibles and write in your journal the spiritual blessings that stick out to you the most. Also, go back through your devotional and write down the 3 days that impacted you the most. Happy Mothering in Christ.

"Who shall separate us from the love of Christ? Shall tribulation, or distress, or persecution, or famine, or nakedness, or danger, or sword?...No, in all these things we are more than conquerors through him who loved us. For I am sure that neither death nor life, nor angels nor rulers, nor things present nor things to come, nor powers, 39 nor height nor depth, nor anything else in all creation, will be able to separate us from the love of God in Christ Jesus our Lord."
—Romans 8:35, 37- 39.

Journal Notes

About the Author

Katie LaPierre is a homeschooling mama of seven children eleven and under. Her husband, Scott, is the senior pastor of Woodland Christian Church, an author, and conference speaker. They grew up together in northern California, and they currently reside in Woodland, Washington.

You can contact Katie or learn more about her at the following:

- Email: mrs.scottlapierre@gmail.com
- Website: www.katielapierre.org
- Facebook: @eternallymindedmamas
- Instagram: @eternallymindedmamas

Newsletter Subscription

To receive the most recent news about Katie and her writing, please subscribe to her husband's newsletter:

https://subscribe.scottlapierre.org/

Would You Like to Invite Scott to Speak at Your Event?

You can expect:

- Professionally prepared and delivered messages
- Handouts with lessons and discussion questions
- Copies of Pastor Scott's and Katie's books to offer as gifts to increase registrations (if you desire)
- Prompt replies to communication
- Advertising of your event on Pastor Scott's and Katie's social media

Schedule for Conferences—Typically there are one or two sessions on Friday evening, and three or four sessions on Saturday, but there is flexibility: conferences can be spread over three days or kept to one day, and Q&A sessions can be added.

Outreach—Consider viewing the conference as an outreach to share Christ with your community. Pastor Scott can run a Facebook ad, and/or set up a Facebook event page for those in the church to share with others.

For more information, including sample messages and endorsements, please visit:

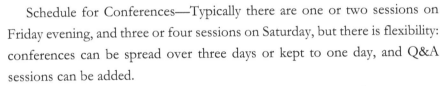

www.scottlapierre.org/conferences-and-speaking.

Marriage God's Way:
A Biblical Recipe for Healthy, Joyful, Christ-Centered Relationships

Nearly everything in life comes with instructions, from the cell phones we use to the automobiles we drive. Yet when it comes to marriage, many people struggle without proper guidance. Pastor Scott presents the needed biblical instructions combined with:

- Personal stories and application to daily life
- Explanations of the roles and responsibilities God has given husbands and wives
- Answers to common questions about godly love and how to show it, headship and submission, intimacy, and establishing an indestructible foundation for your relationship

Endorsed by well-known ministry leaders:

- **Tedd Tripp**: "The reader will be richly rewarded." —Best-selling author of *Shepherding a Child's Heart*
- **Scott Brown**: "This is what every marriage needs!" —Founder of The National Center for Family-Integrated Churches and author of *A Theology of the Family*

Enduring Trials God's Way:
A Biblical Recipe for Finding Joy in Suffering

Trials are part of life on this side of heaven, and God wants to use them for your good! Learn scriptural principles that give you the encouragement you need when suffering. Every chapter concludes with questions that help you apply what you are reading.

- Develop the spiritual perspective to embrace trials
- Appreciate the maturity trials produce
- Understand the rewards for enduring trials
- Recognize God is still compassionate and gracious during trials

Enduring Trials God's Way has been endorsed by well-known ministry leaders:

- **Douglas Bond:** "Richly biblical and encouraging, Scott LaPierre's latest book reveals a gracious pastor's heart, compassionately equipping people for trials. Every believer needs this book!"
  —Speaker, tour leader, and author
- **Dr. Carlton McLeod:** "One of the best biblical treatments of suffering I have seen. You want this book in your library!"
  —Speaker, author, and senior pastor

A Father Offers His Son:
The True and Greater Sacrifice Revealed Through Abraham and Isaac

Have you ever wondered why God asked Abraham to sacrifice his son in Genesis 22? The Angel stopped Abraham showing God did not intend for him to kill Isaac, but what did God desire? God wanted to test Abraham, and readers will discover the account primarily reveals:

- In human terms what God would do with His Son two thousand years later
- The many ways Abraham and Isaac are a picture of God and His Son
- The tremendous love of God shown through Christ's sacrifice

Genesis 22 is not primarily about Abraham and Isaac. God and Jesus are the true and greater Father and Son shining forth in the account. Abraham did not spare his son but was willing to deliver him up for God. Likewise, God "did not spare His Son, but delivered Him up for us all" (Romans 8:32).

Learn the remarkable parallels between God and Abraham, and Jesus and Isaac. With thought-provoking questions at the end of each chapter, the book is perfect for personal use or small groups.

A Father Offers His Son has been endorsed by ministry leaders:

- **Dr. Paul Benware:** "I highly recommend this work that will deepen your appreciation for what the Father and Son went through. The excellent insights will encourage your soul."
  —Professor, Pastor, Speaker, and Author
- **Cary Green:** "As a jeweler holds a gemstone and examines each priceless, shining facet, Pastor Scott holds high this picture of heaven's sacrificial love and examines every detail."
  —Senior Pastor, Missionary, and Church Planter

Notes

i "G1377 - diōkō."–

https://www.blueletterbible.org/lang/lexicon/lexicon.cfm?Strongs=G1377&t=ESV

ii Clarkson, Sally. "Practicing Believing and Walking in Faithfulness." August 8, 2017.

http://sallyclarkson.com/blog/2017/4/11/practicing-believing-and-walking-in-faithfulness

iii Swinnock, George. https://christianquote.com/tag/george-swinnock/page/2/

iv Tozer, A.W. http://blogs.christianpost.com/christianlife/can-your-business-ministry-or-marriage-dare-to-fail-2991/

v "G5219 – hypakouō,"

https://www.blueletterbible.org/lang/lexicon/lexicon.cfm?Strongs=G5219&t=ESV

vi "G5293 – hypotassō."

https://www.blueletterbible.org/lang/lexicon/lexicon.cfm?Strongs=G5293&t=ESV

vii "G4550 – sapros."

https://www.blueletterbible.org/lang/lexicon/lexicon.cfm?Strongs=G4550&t=ESV

viii "H6869 – tsarah."

https://www.blueletterbible.org/lang/lexicon/lexicon.cfm?Strongs=H6869&t=ESV

ix "G1933 - epieiks."

https://www.blueletterbible.org/lang/lexicon/lexicon.cfm?Strongs=G1933&t=ESV

Made in the USA
San Bernardino, CA
31 January 2019